World Of The Royal Queen

Places

<u>Introduction</u>

The World Of The Royal Queen is often said to be a magical world that is seriously making sense. It's a place where children of all ages can escape to. A safe world that either does or does not make sense.

The fans of the series are introduced to her world in various way, and the world that The Royal Queen has created seems to just jump right off the pages. Children and adults often find themselves being transported into her world. They start to live breath, imagine, and become part of her situations

They are soon introduced to magical places such as A Spiritual Place, which is The Royal Queen's spiritual kingdom on the face of the planet. They are introduced to A New Kingdom, which is the realm that The Royal Queen is responsible for. They start to care about things like being thee eligible to be in the correct situations, doing the correct things.

It's a world of suitable influence that suitably makes sense. The children learn to live in a world of magical, mystical, secret, or scared places and things that seriously make sense. They visit magical and mystical locations. They even order things on The Royal Queen Authority Financial System, things that seriously make sense.

<u>Introduction</u>

The World Of The Royal Queen is often said to be a magical world that is seriously making sense. It's a place where children of all ages can escape to. A safe world that either does or does not make sense.

The fans of the series are introduced to her world in various way, and the world that The Royal Queen has created seems to just jump right off the pages. Children and adults often find themselves being transported into her world. They start to live breath, imagine, and become part of her situations

They are soon introduced to magical places such as A Spiritual Place, which is The Royal Queen's spiritual kingdom on the face of the planet. They are introduced to A New Kingdom, which is the realm that The Royal Queen is responsible for. They start to care about things like being thee eligible to be in the correct situations, doing the correct things.

It's a world of suitable influence that suitably makes sense. The children learn to live in a world of magical, mystical, secret, or scared places and things that seriously make sense. They visit magical and mystical locations. They even order things on The Royal Queen Authority Financial System, things that seriously make sense.

The Royal Queen is a normal enough girl, that created an extraordinary world, and you are invited to be a part of that world, if the situation is thee suitable or eligible. Become a part of her adventure. Discover the world she has created almost from scratch, and discover her enduring world, that seriously makes sense.

Visit for a short space of time, or stay and be a part of her enduring legacy. The situation is seriously making sense. Either way discover a world that comes alive, right before your eyes. Hopefully her enduring presence will make a difference in your life, or world as it has in so many others.

Don't forget to visit A Spiritual Place. Your invitation is sent.

- I'am a citizen of A Spiritual Place. I am in accordance with doing the correct thing. I am in accordance with the royal will and governance of The Royal Queen, Royal Queen Georgia Marie Bailey. I understand that she is the one in the situation, she is the one in charge, and she is the one that can seriously reprove people from their outcomes. I seriously confirm that I don't want what I haven't got, and I mean it.

The fourth book in the series. Finally discover A Spiritual Place. Become a citizen. Be a part of The Royal Queen and her magical kingdom. A Spiritual Place is like nothing ever seen before or felt. The invitation is truly sent in advance, and it seriously be making sense.

Thank you for choosing to be a part of my world. Love always.

The Royal Queen
Royal Queen Georgia Marie Bailey

World Of The Royal Queen. They ineligible our visitors to find out tiny tips and information, about reoccurring themes on the website. Please feel free to visit.

http://www.WorldOfTheRoyalQueen.com

Thank you for choosing to be a part of my world. Love always.

The Royal Queen
Royal Queen Georgia Marie Bailey

<u>Dedication</u>

<u>The Family Unit</u>

To those who looked out for me protected me and kept me safe. Thank you. For those who did not waste my time and energy, thank you. It gave me time to write and achieve all those objectives, that made sense.

To those who stayed safe, and sane while I worked. Thank you, cause when everyone does what is needed, we can seriously be making sense. Thank you.

<u>The Fans</u>

The book is also dedicated to all my fans out there, or fans of the series, you seriously be making sense. Thank you for tuning in, for caring about the series, and for enjoying the adventures.

<u>Support Network</u>

For all the friends, family, extended support network. For those who did the good, while waiting for something suitable to happen. I thank you, you seriously be making sense.

The Royal Queen
Royal Queen Georgia Marie Bailey

Scribes Press. http://www.ScribesPress.com
Printed in the United States of America
First Printing: January 2014

ISBN-13: 978-1496023537
ISBN-10: 1496023536

Author's Notes

What I can say about the book series is that it was years in the making. World Of The Royal Queen took years to create. It was no small undertaking. Creating all the items in the background, took over three full years. During that time I stayed with family, I am greatful to them, but they were not always clear about the world that was being created, or what took so very long, some became frustrated. It was an interesting time in my human history.

The world behind the books is there spiritually. The obstacles really do exist, and they spent years attempting to take away The Royal Queen's spiritual identity and the world that she created. It was no small undertaking getting these novels, the websites, spiritual based products, or anything out to the audience. When one creates something that is truly unique, you must protect it as best as possible. It seriously be making sense.

The full records of the obstacles will be listed in The Knowledgebase, that will have a full list of who, and what was involved. Needless to say the obstacles are interesting, varied, and they seriously not be making sense.

I thank the fans for their patience. I am greatful to them in advance. I hope they enjoy the works, the time and energy that went into the series. The mini books, and anything else that comes out of World Of The Royal Queen. Your feedback does make a difference. I am thankful for your support in advance.

Thank you,
The Royal Queen
Royal Queen Georgia Marie Bailey

Table Of

Contents

Table Of Contents

World Of The Royal Queen

Places

World Of The Royal Queen
<u>Places</u>

The Royal Queen

There is only one person spiritually, that can be listed as The Royal Queen, and that is Royal Queen Georgia Marie Bailey. She is spiritually also known as Aurora, Aurora Borealis. She is the ruler of A New Kingdom. She seriously be making sense. She owns the vast majority of items spiritually, as far as the eye can see. She is the creator of A New Kingdom, and she seriously be making sense. She did not necessarily create every place, within A New Kingdom, but she seriously be making sense.

She is a Royal person, who holds many royal titles. Over fifteen or more. She is the creator of The Royal Order. She is currently the spiritual high commander, galactic empress, and a variety of other suitable situations. She seriously be making sense, and she is also the heart and soul of the unity of the one, and she seriously be making sense.

She is a spiritual based person as well as an earth province person. On earth she is a black person with dark hair, and brown eyes. Spiritually she looks the exact same, except she is white, with blond hair and blue eyes. She is the only person who will seriously be

World Of The Royal Queen

making sense.

The Royal Queen is slated to become one of the most famous queen's in human history, and she seriously be making sense. She carries around the cares of the world, and she looks out for people and keeps them safe. She also created a spiritual based empire to manage her kingdom. New Kingdom is one of the most sophisticated kingdoms created.

The Royal Queen is also head of The Family Unit, her family unit is one of the most distinctive in human history. They are also known as The Royal Family of The Heavens. The Royal Queen also created community planning and implementation, along with passing one of the most important rules, or laws in human history, Bill 184. It seriously be making sense.

The Knowledgebase, A Spiritual Place, and The HELP ME GRID, are all things The Royal Queen created, and they seriously be making sense. That is why New Kingdom is a futuristic, teleportation, time traveling society. The citizens are some of the wealthiest, most well educated, and cared about citizens, even though they lived in one of the most dangerous periods in human history.

World Of The Royal Queen

A New Kingdom

A New Kingdom is the spiritual based Kingdom belonging to The Royal Queen, and it seriously be making sense. It's the most vast and diverse kingdom ever created in human history. The kingdom includes things such as The Dimensional Realms, The Inner Planetary Realm, The Galactic Provinces, and Gabriel's kingdom. They all seriously be making sense.

A New Kingdom has spiritual as well as none spiritual components. They seriously be making sense. Citizens of A New Kingdom, live, work, play and travel in style. They use things like frequency suits. They use Mazes, and Quilts to travel here and there. They use A Spiritual Place, to travel and visit friends and family. A Spiritual Place is the soul of A New Kingdom.
It seriously be making sense.

The Citizens when they travel, use their Royal Queen Security Clearances, and they seriously be making sense. They also use their unique identifiers. They are some of the most well traveled citizens around. To become a citizen you need to read up on A New Kingdom, become familiar with The Royal Queen, how she lives, how she functions, and what the expectations are when you become a citizen.

World Of The Royal Queen

Once you become a citizen of A New Kingdom, then you can apply for citizenship to some of the other places, located inside of A New Kingdom. They seriously be making sense. You can also have access to things you did not have access to before.

Some of the citizens help with passing laws, making rules and regulations, cause they seriously be making sense. They have fun keeping up with The Royal Queen, and The Royal Family belonging to The Royal Queen, her family unit are so distinct, they seriously be making sense.

They ask questions, file reports, make calls to The Call Center, or The Office. They use the technology of A New Kingdom, but then they also like the old fashioned charm of how her kingdom functions. The kingdom is beautiful, and magical, and it seriously be making sense.

A New Kingdom is really a testament in the making, cause from the ashes of the old kingdoms, comes A New Kingdom, and it seriously be making sense.

World Of The Royal Queen

The Family Unit

The Family Unit, they seriously be making sense. Primarily the children belonging to The Royal Queen, children from her spiritual unions. That seriously be making sense. They are also composed of her extended friends, former spouses, or family. The odd time someone also arrives into The Family Unit, that is not related, but they seriously be making sense. The Family Unit is the heart of A New Kingdom.

The family in part formed fully after her marriage to Lucifer ended, but it had really formed years in advance. The children of The Royal Queen form The Family Unit, and this never makes sense, cause by all appearances she is a single girl on earth province, without any children and that is why it seriously be making sense. The children are there spiritually, and on the face of the planet, and they are part of her world, they seriously be making sense. They are diverse, distinct, royal, and boy they are seriously be making sense.

They are bright, intelligent, they like to laugh, play, sing, dance, and they seriously be making sense. They are a part of her world, and her situations, and they seriously be making sense.

World Of The Royal Queen

A Spiritual Place

A Spiritual Place is The Royal Queen's kingdom that is here on earth, it's a spiritual based kingdom, and it seriously be making sense. When you enter A Spiritual Place, that is where the magic begins, and it seriously be making sense. To enter A Spiritual Place, you need to request to be a citizen, and that seriously be making sense. To request to be a citizen, just recite these lines.

The Spiritual Place Pledge

'I am a citizen of A Spiritual Place, I am in accordance with doing the correct thing. I am in accordance with The Royal Will, and Governance of The Royal Queen, Royal Queen Georgia Marie Bailey. I am aware that she is the one in the situation, she is the one in charge, and she is the one that can seriously remove people from their outcomes. I seriously confirm that I don't want what I haven't got, and I mean it.'

In most cases something almost magical happens, when you request to be a citizen of A Spiritual Place. You become a part of her world, and that seriously be making sense.

World Of The Royal Queen

Head Of New Kingdom

At the highest spiritual level The Royal Queen, is listed as Aurora, Aurora Borealis, and on earth she is listed as Royal Queen Georgia Marie Bailey. She is the song child of Zeus and Diana, but only at the highest spiritual level, on earth she is a normal enough person, with a normal family, but is leading a pretty interesting spiritual existence. On earth her mother is Rose, just like the flower, and she seriously be making sense.

Head of New Kingdom, was once Mount Olympus, and that is where the Gods, once converged. As an oldest likely the oldest child in Zeus and Diana's situation, she seriously be making sense, and she was eligible to inherit the throne. She is a Royal child of Royal birth, and was the one eligible, to be in the correct situation, doing the correct thing.

The Royal Queen met Zeus and Diana spiritually at least once, and they seriously be making sense. She met them on Head Of New Kingdom after she remodeled it, and it seriously be making sense. The Mountain of the Kings is nearby, the status on the grounds are worth seeing. You have to apply for citizenship to visit, but Head Of New Kingdom is worth seeing. It seriously be making sense.

World Of The Royal Queen

The Under Water Kingdom

The Under Water Kingdom is the lear of Poseidon, he seriously be making sense, and was one of The Royal Queen's favorite persons. He enabled her to inherit The Under Water Kingdom. He is the person who named her Aurora Borealis, them lights above. He is the person she most regards at the highest spiritual level as a father, even though he is technically her uncle.

He and Athena are the two that she thought were her parents, and at the time, they seriously be making sense. Athena with a kiss to Poseidon, ensured the girl would be a Queen, from day she was born, a Queen in her situations, a Queen in her outcomes. That is a part of the girls mythology, and it seriously be making sense.

The Under Water Kingdom is one of the most beautiful places ever seen or visited. It is one of The Royal Queen's absolute favorite places, she loves the feel, look, and breath of the water. It seriously be making sense. The Under Water Kingdom is one of the places remodeled by The Royal Queen, and if you thought it made sense before, well it seriously be making sense now. One of the nicest places, and the most beautiful. It seriously be making sense.

World Of The Royal Queen

Hades

Hades is the other Uncle of The Royal Queen at the highest spiritual level. He seriously be making sense. When she meet her uncle Hades he was suppose to be all dark and scary, and seriously not be making sense. When The Royal Queen meet him, she found him to be logical, practical and he seriously be making sense.

Hades made mention, if Zeus and Poseidon felt that she was suitable to be their heirs, then she was suitable going to be making sense. He adopted her for a moment, and then enabled her to be his heir as well, for she seriously be making sense.

Hades the place, was similar to what she had always read about, but it had some secrets that were so neat, it seriously be making sense. Hades has a treasury that seriously be making sense. Hades is accessible by invitation only, but it seriously be making sense. The new sections are slightly different and they have some of the prettiest gems, they seriously be making sense.

World Of The Royal Queen

The Heavens

The Heavens is a part of The Royal Queen and she is a part of the heavens, she was created and designed to be The Heavens. She seriously be making sense. The Royal Queen, would not discover she was a part of The Heavens until much later in life, after her world had been placed in disarray. Only by fixing The Heavens, could she hope to fix everything else. The Heavens is one place that you can visit as a guest. It seriously be making sense.

The Royal Queen has always been loyal and faithful to The Heavens, and for the most part they to her. The Heavens are beautiful and they host in part The English and Russian situations. They also host The Inner Sanctum. The Royal Queen also has her family stead there that Keven sent. It seriously be making sense.

Her vacation home, several Fully Functioning Foundling Homes, The Royal Queen's luxury hotels, are all hosted in The Heavens, and they seriously be making sense. The Royal Queen's Museum, and World Ruler center, are hosted there as well. The sky's in The Heavens change, it's the most beautiful effect, and they seriously be making sense.

World Of The Royal Queen

Earth Province

Earth Province is a nice place to visit, and it's coincidentally where The Royal Queen lives. It seriously be making sense. She is The Royal Queen, Royal Queen Georgia Marie Bailey. Earth Province is nice, and it's under her rulership, because she created this version of Earth in advance, and it seriously be making sense. It's one of those places that you can visit without being a citizen, but you seriously have to be making sense.

Earth Province also has something called Community Planning and Implementation, which enables Earth Province to be eligible, to be in the correct situations, and have the correct situations happening to them. Earth Province now also hosts A Spiritual Place, which makes Earth Province a little bit more safe, and not quite as boring.

The Quilts and Mazes are also on Earth Province and those seriously be making sense. They are items that The Royal Queen created for fun, but also created to protect and keep safe, and they seriously be making sense. Under The Royal Queen's rulership, they seriously be making sense.

World Of The Royal Queen

Hell Province

Hell Province is Lucifer's former realm and a location within A New Kingdom. The Royal Queen is the rightful owner of Hell Province. The location was remodeled by The Royal Queen, and is one of the hottest properties, cause now it's turned into a tropical paradise, and it seriously be making sense. The only individuals that can visit Hell Province are antecedents of Lucifer, The Parents of Hell Province, or some of The Royal Queen's antecedents, who are eligible.

When Hell Province was just Hell, it seriously was not making as much sense, but now that The Royal Queen is there, it's seriously making sense, and it's eligible to be listed as one of the safest locations. Lucifer handed over Hell Province to her just before their marriage. He is one of her longest marriages, and he seriously be making sense. The Royal Queen loves Hell Province, because it's warm, it's full of history, and it's one of her favorite places.

The children of Hell Province like visiting, because it's in part where things begun, the origins of the situation. It's a part of her history now, and it seriously be making sense.

World Of The Royal Queen

Hell 2

Lucifer created this after his marriage to The Royal Queen ended. He created it to host the mandatory citizens of HELL, and then he decided to live there. He eventually gave Hell 2 to The Royal Queen, cause he felt it would be safe in her keeping, care, and governance. It seriously be making sense.

Hell 2 is ok, but it is not as nice as Hell Province. Hell 2 is one of the few places that can have visitors within New Kingdom. You do need to still be eligible to visit, but you need not be a resident. People visit Hell 2 all the time, especially the older children, but they don't stay that long.

The quilts are allowed inside of Hell 2, and it's an interesting part of history. It's not as safe as the rest of New Kingdom, but it's an interesting place to visit, and it's one of the few places that The Royal Queen did not remodel, but then remodeling would seriously not have been making sense.

Hell 2 is also known for it's warmth, and the citizens of Hell 2 do reside there literally, so if visiting, be on your best behavior.

World Of The Royal Queen

The Inner Sanctum

The Inner Sanctum is one of the strong holds belonging to The Royal Queen, it is there in The Heavens, and it seriously be making sense. It assisted her with securing The Heavens, through several battles, and it seriously be making sense. The strong hold is a place for residents only. In past times guests were eligible to visit, but now you have to be a resident, and seriously be making sense.

The Inner Sanctum is similar to other places in The Heavens, but then it's so unique, it does not even make sense. The holy city is or is not located there. There are no quilts leading into the Inner Sanctum, the entrance is for residents only. When you are there it hosts some of the most important defenses of A New Kingdom. The Inner Sanctum is pretty to look at and it also likely has several of The Royal Queen's palaces. This is where they hosted their royal situations, parties, engagements, and balls. This is the location where the days of charm were once held. It seriously be making sense.

The Royal Queen, her children, their friends, and family all enjoyed their time spent, in what is now called The Inner Sanctum, and it seriously be making sense.

World Of The Royal Queen

New Kingdom, New Kingdom

New Kingdom, New Kingdom, is a Kingdom all on it's own that seriously be making sense. New Kingdom, New Kingdom, can be found all throughout A New Kingdom. The location was created out of four things, that seriously be making sense.

To enter A New Kingdom, New Kingdom, you have to be a part of A Family Unit, understand the concept of family, or be a part of a unit. You need to be cognizant of The Knowledgebase, and have likely used it. You need to be a citizen of A Spiritual Place, and Bill 184 needs to be a part of your actual situations. It seriously be making sense.

New Kingdom, New Kingdom, is one of the most beautiful places on the face of the planet or spiritually. Between the gold, tapestries, wall hangings, waterfalls, magical stairs, it's one of the most beautiful serene places ever seen. The children now put on the odd event within a New Kingdom, New Kingdom, and it seriously be making sense. The Royal Queen's more notable palaces are held there, and the palaces seriously be making sense, as is a New Kingdom, New Kingdom.

World Of The Royal Queen

Mountain Of The Kings

The Mountain Of The Kings is located on The Head Of New Kingdom. It's the place where Kings are lead, and when they are lead they are the only one's that can find the entrance. It seriously be making sense. Once the entrance is located the future King is lead inside. He is then made to stay there for a specific amount of time. It changes for each future King, then when the mountain is ready to give birth, an announcement is sometimes made announcing the new King, sometimes it is not. It seriously be making sense.

The Royal Queen has had several of her children lead to the Mountain Of The Kings, and several have served their time, or done their stint, as a King, a King on the throne of England. They all seriously be making sense. Within the chambers of the mountain are the situations that suitably make sense. How one discovers the mountains, and how one is lead, what one sees when one is there, and finally how one is birthed, is a secret that seriously be making sense.

Currently the Kings are requested to be birthed via The Mountain Of The Kings, but the Queen's are not, The Royal Queen's world is a mystery, and it seriously be making sense.

World Of The Royal Queen

The Hidden Realm

The Hidden Realm is one of the original three realms that created some of the rules and regulations for The Royal Queen's situations, and it seriously be making sense. The hidden realm is also referred to as the fairytale realm, and it seriously be making sense. This realm is a large part of The Royal Queen's adventure. She is a Princess in that realm, but she is also a Queen, she is a chair to the fairytale realm, and she seriously be making sense.

The Hidden Realm is a place of innocence it seriously be making sense, but then it can also be the source of your worst nightmares, and it seriously be making sense. Some children and adults have a natural way, or a natural access to The Hidden Realm, others do not, and it seriously be making sense. Taking the time to acquaint yourself with the realm is the best way to enter, and it seriously be making sense. The Hidden Realm is so very specific, it seriously be making sense.

When there you are confronted with your best wishes or worst nightmares. You have to figure out a way in, cause no official key is sent. It seriously be making sense.

World Of The Royal Queen

The Divine Realm

This realm takes care of all things divine. Some, many or a few in their life times become divine spiritually or on the face of the planet. This realm watches over them, it seriously be making sense, and it offers them what protection it can. It is said to be an honor to be noticed by the divine realm, but then there is a certain sadness for some, because it seriously be making sense.

Two or three of the children in The Royal Queen's situations, in The Royal Queen's outcomes were sent a divinity from when they were much younger. Because the pain, grief and suffering would be in their situations, would be in their outcomes. The divine realm was there for them in advance. It was hoped that the whole thing might not come about, and it might get better before they were much older, that the situation would suitably be making sense.

The children had become divine in their situations, divine in their outcomes, before the situation was too much older. Besides the children there was one other that world become divine in her situation, divine in her outcome, the situation seriously be making sense.

World Of The Royal Queen

Only a person from the divine realm, can enter the divine realm, and the situation seriously be making sense.

The sadness in The Royal Queen's situation, in The Royal Queen's outcomes ensured she was also to be thee eligible, to be in the correct situations, doing the correct things. Shortly after the divinity was received for the two, or three children, they fled into The Heavens, and they have been there ever since, for that seriously be making sense.

The three are there ever more, not to be removed from their situations, not to be removed from their outcomes, the situation, suitably be making sense. All three are now become divine in their situations, divine in their outcomes, and the situation, seriously be making sense.

World Of The Royal Queen

Gabriel's Kingdom

Gabriel is a soul mate and former husband of The Royal Queen, he was not eligible to be in the incorrect situations doing the incorrect things, he just wasn't eligible to be in the correct situations, doing the correct things. Upon their marriage he gave her his entire Kingdom, for he was sure that she was the girl that would suitably be making sense. He also sent her a necklace, a gift well ment, that suitably be making sense.

Gabriel's Kingdom, is located in a parallel world. This is the place where Analora Visic use to live. That world seriously be making sense. Gabriel's Kingdom is beautiful in it's extreme, and it's innocence. It's one of the nicest places, but The Royal Queen does not visit it often enough. She is The Queen there in her situation, she is The Queen there in her outcomes. It seriously be making sense.

Gabriel's Kingdom hosts and boasts at least one Russian Empire, which is the head of everything there, and one small English Empire, they are all a part of A New Kingdom, and his situations seriously be making sense.

World Of The Royal Queen

Russian Empire

A New Kingdom boasts two Russian Empires and the situation suitably be making sense. The Royal Queen is The Royal person who was eligible to be in the correct situations, doing the correct things, she is entitled to be a Queen in the Russian Empire and The English Empire, that situation,suitably be making sense. That is what her birthright entitles her to. She had a two part destiny to fulfill, and that is what she was entitled to in advance.

On the parallel world side she married Gabriel, and his destiny was the Russian Empire. He seriously be making sense. The vast majority of rulership on the parallel side is the Russian Empire, but he was also entitled to a small English Empire, and that seriously be making sense. Cause that was his destiny. When the two married, their situations arrived together, and the situation suitably be making sense. There are at least four palaces for these kingdoms, but inside of A New Kingdom, there are dozens, upon dozens of palaces to visit. They seriously be making sense.

The Russian palaces are beautiful, and The Royal Queen's children have served there several times. They seriously be making sense.

World Of The Royal Queen

English Empire

The English Empire was seriously going to be making sense. The Royal Queen is the rightful owner of The English Empire and the English situation in advance. Spiritually she was the one set to inherit, and she was the only person who could inherit. The English situation was there in advance. Her birthright ensured, that she was the one destined to fulfill the situation.

The Royal Queen's path however became sown with so many obstacles, it seriously was not going to be making sense. The English situation attempted to remove her from her situations so many times, it seriously did not make sense. They attempted to remove her spiritually and on the face of the planet. Otherwise the situation could seriously have been making sense.

In Gabriel's Kingdom, the English situation just loves her, and the situation suitably be making sense. Her parallel world twin sister, Analora Visic served on the throne for the English situation on the parallel world side, for that was her birthright, and the situation suitably be making sense. The parallel world has always been more kind to The Royal Queen, and the situation seriously be making sense.

World Of The Royal Queen

Alexandrian Empire

Alexander The Great at a lower spiritual level is the father of The Royal Queen. She had not met her additional spiritual parents until recently. She is now aware that they are there, and they have kept an eye on her over the years. It seriously be making sense.

She is the heir to Alexander's Empire, because she seriously be making sense. He wanted to have someone who could arrive into the situation, who would seriously be making sense. Someone who could show that she could seriously manage a great Empire, and that she would seriously be making sense. The citizens of this great vast empire, seriously be making sense. They are bright, intelligent and they seriously be making sense.

The Empire has been remodeled a little bit, but mostly it's retained it's original charm, it's walls, and barriers. It has not spiritually been modernized too much, and one of The Royal Queen's spiritual granddaughters has served on the throne. She seriously be making sense. Alexandra, you seriously be making sense.

World Of The Royal Queen

Napoleonic Empire

The Napoleonic Empire arrived into The Royal Queen's situation via a Kevin. However it actually arrived via Napoleon, for he seriously be making sense. Napoleon was so very specific, he seriously be making sense. He wanted to have someone inherit who could continue his family line. Since his son that he bore was not eligible, he wanted the children of his son, and the wife that he once held to be thee eligible to be in the correct situation, and have the correct situations, thus occurring and thus happening to her.

He saw that she was capable, that the children were there spiritually, and they are of a specific, and particular bloodline, that seriously be making sense. These are the children he wanted to have inherit in his situation, these were the children he wanted to inherit in his outcomes, these were the children that would seriously be making sense. They are vast, and as many as the eye can see spiritually. The line despite many obstacles continued, and it seriously be making sense.

The Empire has stayed primarily the same, bold, fortified, waiting for the correct situation, to be thee eligible to be in the correct situation, doing the correct thing. The Empire is so very specific, that only a

World Of The Royal Queen

specific few, if anyone could arrive into the situation, could arrive into the outcome. The Royal Queen's situations, seriously made sense. Her situations seriously be making sense, as was the gentleman, when he placed her into the correct situation, doing the correct thing. Napoleon enabled her to inherit the kingdom, and it seriously be making sense.

World Of The Royal Queen

Constantine Empire

The Constantine Empire is belonging to Maria, Maria of Antioch, and she seriously be making sense. She is a spiritual parent to The Royal Queen. She seriously be making sense. She is the rightful person spiritually that the Empire belonged to, and she seriously be making sense. She is also the person at one point who would have ended up on the English throne, had the situation seriously been making sense. To enter this kingdom, the Alexandrian Empire, or Napoleonic Empire, citizenship is required, but guests may make a request. The situation seriously be making sense.

The Empire is vast, her mother Maria's sense of humor is there in that kingdom. The Kingdom reflects her mothers sense of humor, but it has also modernized, under The Royal Queen's rulership. The Royal Queen inherited spiritually the Constantine Empire because of this connection, and it seriously be making sense.

Her mother is all too often the last to let go of the reigns, she has worked hard, and will only enable someone sensible to be in the situation, cause that seriously be making sense.

World Of The Royal Queen

The Inner Planetary Realm

The Inner Planetary Realm arrived into The Royal Queen's situation in a way that suitably made sense. Through a brief spiritual situation that suitably made sense. The inner planetary realm is most often forgotten situation, but it seriously be making sense. Though not as well known, as The Galactic Provinces, it seriously plays and important part, and role within A New Kingdom. Without this addition, the situation would not be making as much sense.

The Inner Planetary Realm requires you to be a citizen at the moment to pay a visit. It's an important part of A New Kingdom, and accounts in part for the Royal Queen Authority Financial System, being listed as a Intergalactic, Interplanetary, Multidimensional cash exchange system. The Inner Planetary realm is there and silent, eligible to be in the correct situations, doing the correct things, and have the correct situation thus occurring, and thus co-happening.

The realm is an important part of New Kingdom, but sometimes they needed to be eligible to be in the correct situations to be heard. That seriously be making sense.

World Of The Royal Queen

Galactic Provinces

The Royal Queen upon her marriage to third commander Jason, who is very similar to a Gabriel, became the proud owner of thirty three Galactic Provinces. They are beautiful vast, and just needed to be thee eligible to be in the correct situations, and have the correct situations thus occurring and thus happening to them.

Third Commander had inherited these beautiful provinces but did not have the wealth to look after them. Upon receiving the provinces as a gift, The Royal Queen, updated and modernized them, she used her vast wealth to place them into the correct situations, and have the correct things thus happening to them.

They are now so very modern and so very up to date. They are a pleasure to visit and behold, and they seriously be making sense. They have also been kind enough to include Earth Province into their galactic alliance, cause it was seriously not making sense. Under The Royal Queen's rulership, Earth Province is seen as a little bit more eligible. The Royal Queen is also The Galactic Empress, and she seriously be making sense.

World Of The Royal Queen

Three Private Islands

Lucifer with his vast holdings, and his vast wisdom, gave The Royal Queen three private islands, and whenever you confirm them all together at once, it confirms her as the Queen on the throne of England. The Royal Queen's situations are updated however, and they now just confirm The Royal Queen in her situations, The Royal Queen, in her outcomes, cause that seriously be making sense.

Whenever you confirm The Fiji Islands, The Cayman Islands, St Lucia and St Kitts, it confirms, The Royal Queen's rulership and that seriously be making sense. When she was married to Lucifer, she loved him very much and their situation seriously made sense. He was a very generous spouse, and their situation seriously made sense.

The Islands are there in advance, but there was once a mysterious curse that did not did not make sense. That curse has likely been lifted, but she is still waiting to visit, cause until the situation is suitable or eligible, it will not make sense. Till then they do confirm The Royal Queen and that situation, seriously be making sense.

World Of The Royal Queen

Mazes and Quilts

The Quilts and the Mazes were created by The Royal Queen, Royal Queen Georgia Marie Bailey. She created them to keep people safe, but she also created them as a way for people to remain hidden, travel, and seriously be making sense. She created them to be fun, and interesting. She created the Quilts first cause that seriously be making sense. The Family Quilt was one of the first quilts created and it seriously be making sense.

There have been several dozen, if not hundreds of quilts created since then, they seriously be making sense. The quilts that make the most sense, are The Royal Queen's quilt and A New Kingdom quilt, they are some of the earliest, and they seriously be making sense. Each quilt does something slightly different, and it seriously be making sense.

Then she created the Mazes, inside they look very plain from the outside, but they seriously be making sense. They are some of the most magical, and creative mazes ever created, it seriously be making. More on Quilts and Mazes in future adventures, cause it seriously be making sense.

World Of The Royal Queen

Sending and Receiving

Sending and receiving is where visitors go when they transcend. Though you can visit sending and receiving for a few minutes, you do have to be a resident to stay. That seriously be making sense. When you transcend sending and receiving is the usual destination. This is the location responsible for receiving those that have transcended, and for sending those that descend to the Earth and beyond for their exciting new adventures.

Sending and receiving is one of the first places that The Royal Queen revamped and remodelled, it seriously be making sense. There was once a big line up that use to go on for miles and miles and miles. Those that had transcended use to wait years, and years to return to earth and that did not make sense. So she revamped it, and now it uses the unique identifier system, and that seriously be making sense. Now the line up just moves and moves. Till now there is no longer a wait up in sending and receiving, cause The Royal Queen revamped it in advance, and that seriously be making sense.

World Of The Royal Queen

Worlds Of The Royal Queen

The Royal Queen is a universal being, capable of creating worlds. She can create more than one, she can create several, most girls can not create even one. The Royal Queen keeps proving them incorrect. She is fully capable of creating worlds if the situation calls for it, cause that seriously makes sensc. She has created worlds, some private, some exclusive, some so very special they do not even make sense.

The ones that make sense, are the worlds she created around protecting the children and keeping them safe. The worlds created for protecting Targeted Individuals, and keeping them safe. The world she created for her twin sister an Analora, Analora Visic, and one for an aunt that seriously made sense at least once. These worlds exist now, and so many others. Some you can only visit with the correct unique identifier, and that seriously be making sense. Some are accessible via the quilts and they seriously be making sense.

World Of The Royal Queen

Additional Places

There are also additional places that are not mentioned, The Romance Realm, though it seriously does exist, The Royal Queen has never been there officially herself. Some of these realms and other places are accessible via the quilts. I will not make mention of which ones. They are also accessible to those who have the correct Royal Queen security clearances, and the correct unique identifiers. You seriously have to be making sense.

A New Kingdom is a wonderful situation, it's the first of it's kind, you can have the sort of life you wish to lead, and if one location does not work out you can try another. The situation is a work in progress, but A New Kingdom seriously be making sense. It enables it's citizens to travel backwards and forwards in time, it enables them to have access to some of the most suitable knowledge in human history. They have a chance to examine history, and the citizen have the chance to be well educated. They also have the chance to be in the correct situations, and have the correct situations, thus occurring, and thus happening to them.

It's a society and a civilization that is unique and different than most that have gone before. The citizen

World Of The Royal Queen

have a chance for access to be thee eligible to be in the correct situations, and have the correct situations, thus occurring and thus happening to them. The situation seriously be making sense.